TRUST

Falk Richter

TRUST

translated by Maja Zade

OBERON BOOKS
LONDON

WWW.OBERONBOOKS.COM

First published in the English language in 2018 by Oberon Books Ltd
521 Caledonian Road, London N7 9RH
Tel: +44 (0) 20 7607 3637 / Fax: +44 (0) 20 7607 3629
e-mail: info@oberonbooks.com
www.oberonbooks.com

A catalogue record for this book is available from the British Library.

PB ISBN: 9781786823168
E ISBN: 9781786823175

Note

Sections in italics English by Falk Richter
and performed in English in the Schaubühne production.

I

The Searchers

And if I left you it wouldn't change anything

And if I stayed it wouldn't change anything

And if you looked at me it wouldn't change anything

And if you just sat there it wouldn't change anything

Look at you

(Laughs.)

I mean

I mean

Just look at you

This

This

This body or whatever

This is meant to be

I can't do this

You know

I can't do this anymore

I just can't fucking do this anymore

What is he telling me

What is he trying

He, him, this thing

To tell me

I don't get it

Sorry

But

I'm sorry but

Maybe it's better if you just stay over there and I

I don't know

What was I going to say?

What was I going to say?

What am I trying to say?

What do I actually want?

I don't know

I can't remember

And if I touched you it wouldn't change anything

And if I really, really wanted you it wouldn't change anything

We've made it this far

Ten years

My God

I'm sorry

I'm so sorry

Forget everything I said

Let's just leave things the way they are

We've

This equilibrium

This poise

This balance, is that what you call it?

Found this equilibrium and

I I I

I err

I

Err I

Err err err

Too complicated

Let's just leave things the way they are

It's too complicated to change now

Please

I'm so sorry

Forget what I said

I'm sorry

I didn't mean it

Let's just leave things the way they are

Let's not mess everything up now

It took such a long time to get all this

It was so so

Exhausting

(Laughs.)

It's about me

It's not about you

I'm sorry

somehow it's in me and

I'm sorry

this is all my

this is all my I mean this is

I'm sorry

o God

This is me

And this is you

o God

And I

I don't even know

o God

but let's just leave things the way they are

It took such a long time to get this this this *this*

Let's just leave things like this, yes?

Okay?

Good.

I'm sorry.

And what am I supposed to say about this?

It's just that… it's just that this has nothing to do with me, it's your problem

I'm supposed to-?

Yes, why?

Well, what?

Okay, listen

We'll

We'll just leave it like this, we'll just leave it like this

It's taken us ten years to get here, to this point

And now it's just too

No

Have a seat

Too, right?, complicated, to start over again, I mean

You and I and *(laughs)*

Oh dear

I just can't change

I mean

anyway

I mean we've been talking about it for so long and it doesn't change anything

And I really don't get it either

I mean I really can't figure out what you're doing, what you've turned into in the last few years, what's it all about?

Right? I don't know

How, what?

I mean, somehow

Nothing

I don't know either

This is me now

How am I supposed to figure this out? I don't get it

You should figure it out by yourself

I mean we've been working at it for so long that you have to slowly start to

I mean you have to

I can't always be the one who

And you've gotten really old as well

We've been, what?, how long?

Together or whatever you want to call it, yes

by now you should be able to figure it out by yourself

I mean it's not the first

What's all this about?

I don't get it

I can't figure it out

Your movements, this, this body, I mean have you ever actually thought about your body, what it tells you, the story of your body, the story your body tells me every morning

O God, I mean

I don't know

I don't mean any of the things I'm saying, I don't mean anything, I mean I don't know

Maybe there's something wrong with

This is just all too

And it's too exhausting and regardless of, okay, okay

Listen

You're living your life, I'm living my life,

You're here, I'm here

And sometimes it can be nice

Okay, I'm sorry,

I didn't mean it

I didn't mean any of it

What *do* I mean?

What do I mean?

What am I trying to tell you?

I don't know what I'm trying to say.

I, we

I, I'm at a loss

I mean I don't know

This thing

Standing there

Quite pretty really

But somehow

No connection no

But we'll leave it like this, right?

We'll just leave it

We'll just leave it there

We'll just carry on, okay?

Let me

I'm just

There's something

I mean

With me, it's, I think it's just because of, about, I mean I think, yes, me and I'm sorry

Okay

It has nothing to do with you

It's just about me

All this is not about you

All this is just about me

Okay

And if I told you, it wouldn't change anything

And if I didn't tell you, it wouldn't change anything

And if I loved you, it wouldn't change anything

And if we stayed together, it wouldn't change anything

And if I left you, it wouldn't change anything

And if I packed my bags, it would also not change anything

And if I call you, it doesn't change anything

And if I don't call you, it doesn't change anything

And if I kiss you, it doesn't change anything

And if I really, really want you, it doesn't change anything

And if I, if I just fall asleep, it doesn't change anything

And if I fuck you, it doesn't change anything

And if I trust you, I, I, you know, I, yeah, I, I, I, I just can't, I just cannot, I, I, I

I, I, I just cannot trust you

I, I, I, I just, I just can't, I just can't

I don't know, I don't know

I don't know what to say

I don't know the thing is, the thing is that

It is

I don't know

I just, I don't, I just don't, you know, it is, I mean, what

What is this, what is this, what is this

What is this thing, what is this thing with you? Just don't know

Just go and let me sleep

Just go and let me sleep

JUST GO AND LET ME SLEEP

Sorry, sorry it is all my fault

I didn't mean any word of what I said

I didn't mean any word no I didn't I just I don't know sorry I just

I didn't mean that

I am sorry

sorry

And if I told you it wouldn't change anything

And if I didn't tell you it wouldn't change anything

And if I loved you it wouldn't change anything

And it we stayed together it wouldn't change anything

And if I packed my bags it wouldn't change anything

And if I call you it doesn't change anything

And if I don't call you it doesn't change anything

And if I kiss you it doesn't change anything

And if I really, really want you it doesn't change anything

And if I, if I fall asleep now it doesn't change anything

(Pause.)

And if I leave it doesn't change anything

And if I just stand by the window it doesn't change anything

And if I just say yes for once it doesn't change anything

And if I just understand you for one minute it doesn't change anything

Pack your things and stay

stay

And if I trust you, if I, when I

And when I

When I

I just can't

I just

O my God

I really can't do this

I'm so sorry

Forget what I said

I'm sorry

I'm so sorry

I didn't mean it

Let's just leave things the way they are

Let's not mess everything up

All this has taken so long

It was so so

Exhausting

It's only about me

It's not about you

Somehow it's in me and

This is all my

This is all my, I mean this is

O God

This is me

And this is you

O God

And I

I can't do this

And if I touch you it doesn't change anything

And if I really, really want you it doesn't change anything

O God

But let's just leave things the way they are

The Fourth Generation

Every now and then everyone makes music together.
Everyone plays an instrument and those with a good voice
sing.

Judith for example sings a loungey Bossa Nova version of
the Pet Shop Boys' Love etc that sounds as if Kay hears it on
the radio on a taxi ride from Charles de Gaulle airport to the
video archive on the fifth floor of the Centre Pompidou, where
he will spend the day with a coffee and a croissant watching
videos of small children with pale, almost-dead faces gently
leaning against enormous computers and looking blank,
just staring blankly into space and listening to a computer
voice which at irregular intervals speaks a random series of
sentences in the brightly-lit, sterile room:

There is more to life than laundry

The crystal rabbit

The shape of time to come

High Profile

The simple truth about dish washing

One free phone call

And bring you free choice

The fine art of snacking

Kay briefly glances at the installation and remembers the nights of a long journey through a Norwegian fjord landscape with his childhood friend Beate during which they had put Björk's HUMAN BEHAVIOUR on repeat until the argument broke out which released too much pent-up dissatisfaction and eroded the love affair that had only been going for three months and which made Beate – at half past one in the morning, at a motorway service station near Trömseflössn where the sun refused to go down and jumped along the horizon like a table tennis ball, full of rage and with a final slamming of the door – say: "Kay, you're such a loser, you have no idea" and to climb into another driver's car, a good-looking, tall, blond eighteen-year old boy who together with his friends had just won the intermediate round cup of the Trömseflössn handball championship and had now, on his way home, completely drunk from their excessive victory celebrations, made a short stop at the motorway service station because he'd felt ill and needed to throw up, and who without protest handed the steering wheel of his Mitsubishi Colt to Beate, Kay watched them drive away and quietly and without will or resistance thought: "cunt, silly, stupid, fucking fuck crap fucking cunt" and got into his car, where he listened to Judith's voice on the radio, which was whispering rather than singing "YOU NEED MORE THAN A GERHARD RICHTER HANGING ON YOUR WALL", no, that's not right, he doesn't hear Judith's breathy voice singing "too much of anything is never enough" until he gets back into the taxi to return to Charles de Gaulle airport to continue his journey to Shanghai, why Shanghai, we'll explain that later. First Kay has to go past a vast, enormous, expansive collection of sofas, a sofa-and-armchair installation, there are people holding art books in front of their bodies lying on them, they all seem to have fallen asleep reading large art books and works of philosophy and social science: Alain Ehrenberg The Weariness of the Self Eva Illouz Saving the Modern Soul Wolfgang Fritz Haug A Critique of Commodity Aesthetics: Appearance, Sexuality and Advertising in Capitalist Society Byung-Chul Han Hyperculturalism, Culture and

Globalisation, they're all lying here in a sea of sofas and armchairs surging with exhaustion, they're moving slowly, like fern, backwards and forwards, something strange is built into this sofa landscape, it seems to be breathing, it's moving, very slowly, and if you close your eyes and listen to your own breathing you can hear sentences from the books that are lying closed or open on the chests of each sleeping person. Kay lies down, his body wants to become part of this landscape of bodies, he puts a brown bag next to him on the sofa, for him the breathing of all these people is a sea and he is now watching a glowing orange sunset. IN THE MIDDLE OF LIFE part one, that's the name of the book which is suddenly lying open on his chest and is quietly speaking to him, arrived IN THE MIDDLE OF LIFE in the middle of life, I'm now going to rest with these bodies, and he leans back and breathes slowly and suddenly he's surprised, when he closes his eyes there are images and memories, bits of sentences, slowly he starts to doze and swims out into the sea and stays there and keeps swimming further and further towards the orange sunset. And now we're descending the five escalators while Paris is glowing in the July evening sun in his place, we're walking towards the driver who really has been waiting for us all these years, get into the taxi in order to return to the airport so we can catch the night flight to Shanghai to meet the Japanese-Icelandic sociologist Atsushi Lyngursvötsson to revise the new edition of his currently five-volume COLLAPSING SYSTEMS about the collapse of the Roman Empire to the collapse of Soviet socialism, because by the year 2010 this large-scale, meticulously researched examination which has become a standard university text is supposed to be expanded to a sixth volume, THE COLLAPSE OF THE FINANCIAL SYSTEM IN HIGH TECH CAPITALISM AFTER THE COLLAPSE OF SOVIET SOCIALISM, but first of all we need to clarify if our system, like Soviet socialism, will have disappeared in the next five to ten years, whether it will have been replaced and if yes, by what new system. So we get into the taxi feeling slightly unsettled and ask the driver to turn up the radio because Judith is singing

„You need more, you need more, you need more, you need
more you need LOVE" and reread our notes for the
impending meeting to which every significant social scientist,
popular scientist, philosopher, ecologist and systems analyst
from across the world has been invited in order to clarify the
question of whether our current system is already in the
process of collapsing, whether we will now experience its
disintegration or whether this crisis is a purely cyclical
manifestation inherent to the system which from now on will
keep recurring at increasingly short intervals since our system
is at core based on the creation of virtual values and the
destruction of real values, and since the clash will recur
cyclically, these so-called value clashes will keep happening
and fictional, virtual values will simply dissolve since they
never existed in the first place, weren't based on anything real
and hence will just disappear like a mirage, an acid trip or a
manic phase which is then transformed into a phase of
depression, of exhaustion, of rest, collecting oneself, gathering
oneself, which can make you just lie there for a few years
without knowing what you want, what you are capable of, who
you are, you just lie there and do nothing, like an intern who is
lying underneath the rubble of a collapsed high-rise, for
example the collapsed Cologne town archive, or has been hit
by a roof slate Hartmut Mehdorn put on the Berlin Central
Station to deliberately endanger people's lives in order to save
a few Euros which he then transferred to his own account, and
is waiting for a rescue team or a rescue fund which will free
him from the rubble and pull him back into daylight, but
you're waiting and waiting and breathing, exhausted, can't
move and you don't know what to do and you just lie there
and the pain increases and decreases and no one is coming
because the town can no longer afford a rescue team since the
overly-rash SPD city council has used up all the town money
in an unfortunate, ill-considered cross border leasing deal with
the lawyers from Stanley Morgan, we know that, we've read
all about it, it's hard to understand how these people, who are
merely meant to manage the town and whose job it is to make
sure everything runs reasonably smoothly are suddenly acting

like a bunch of out-of-control teenagers on alcopops and running from one American law firm to the next in order to sell everything the town has to offer in terms of material value in overly-complex, incomprehensible contract agreements which are much thicker than the soon-to-be six-volume work by the Japanese-Icelandic social systems analyst Atsushi Lyngursvötsson and which have never been read by anyone in the whole world, in order to later, as it now turns out, to rebuy them at the tenfold price. And we drive past a group of protesters in their mid-fifties, all of them employees of a financially-troubled department store, who are silently holding large banners that say "We're the heart of the city centre. Don't let us die!" that point to the imminent collapse of a large chain of department stores, we're slightly confused because we can still remember a time when people were aggressively campaigning AGAINST these places, these "materialist temples of a bastard inhuman system", and our taxi driver draws us into a conversation about whether the former CEO might have the same motives as those young Baader-Meinhof Group activists that threw a large-scale fire bomb at this department store that was nowhere near as successful as the skilfully-initiated and carefully-planned destruction project of the CEO who, as our taxi driver tells us, flogged the store-owned property to a fund he himself owned and then re-let the same property to the company at an utterly horrendous price which resulted in the company's money draining away while the deftly redirected streams of money went directly into his own account and he, wittingly or unwittingly, had made a much more important contribution to the collapse of the so-called "bastard system" than the Baader-Meinhof Group had ever dared to imagine. "The Fourth Generation," that's the title of the book our taxi driver is working on, and it proposes the daring theory that the Baader-Meinhof Group has worked its way through these institutions and arrived in the leadership of companies and financial institutions and will efficiently and permanently cause this despicable system to go under, and that the collapse of this department store was their first great success.

But we are now going to leave this setting, we're not going to read Atsushi Lyngursvötsson's book COLLAPSING SYSTEMS together, that would go too far, and we might not even understand his book, and even if we did we wouldn't know what to do with all that knowledge. We would be afraid that Atsushi Lyngursvötsson had concluded that the system as we know it will collapse in five years at the latest, and then what would we do with this information? Agree on a new system? How would we do that? Would we all sit down together and talk about what we really need or not and what a happy, fulfilling life could look like which also takes into account people on other continents who are far from being sick of luxury and don't even have water, let alone mobiles, burnouts or divorce lawyers?

Let's just leave things the way they are

It's too complicated to change it now

Let's not cause confusion everywhere

It's taken us so long to get here

It was so so

Exhausting

Let's turn up the radio and listen to Judith singing.

Trust Me

Trust me. Yes, I know I've cheated on you, but I won't do it
again, really, honest, starting from tonight, after everything
that's happened, you can really trust me. Yes, I know I took
the car keys from your bedside table and crashed the car into
a tree with Fred and your account is empty now, I'm sorry,
but I had all these debts because Fred is just so expensive,
but sex with you was just so dull these past few years and
Fred was somehow, I don't know, so different, so powerful
somehow and he had so much time and when he didn't there
was always Alfredo or Dominik or Francesco and they were
all so expensive and they all wanted cars so I gave them
yours, I mean three of the four, one is still left, was left, on
the way over here today I forgot it, err, somewhere or sold
it, I can't remember, or just left it because there was a traffic
jam but, but that will change, honest, TRUST ME, starting
from tomorrow morning or let's say tomorrow noon at the
latest everything is going to change, I'll restrain myself and
be more careful so this kind of thing won't happen any more,
really, yes I know I shouldn't have slept with your brother
but it won't happen again either, no, not with your father and
err, that you got the clap as well and that your computer is
somehow, well, how shall I put it, gone, I'm really sorry about
that, but starting from tomorrow noon or the evening of the
day after tomorrow at the latest, this won't happen again, I've
changed, honest, I've really changed, well, at least I want to, I
really want to, darling, err, could you lend me some money,
well, maybe four billion or something, I'll pay you back, but
otherwise I really can't live, this time I won't get drunk and
toss it in the loo and flush it like the last five billion, honest,
I've changed, I've been thinking and I think I really behaved
badly and I'm sorry, well, err, I'll just go on a short trip for err
three weeks with Tim and err Michael but after that, after that
I'll, like I said, by Monday afternoon in three weeks' time I'll
be a completely new person and everything will be different
and I'll take better care of the two of us because I want you
to be happy with me, to be content AND TO TRUST ME

YOU SHOULD BE ABLE TO TRUST ME AGAIN THAT'S
IMPORTANT TO ME BECAUSE YOU CAN'T LIVE
WITHOUT TRUST okay, well, so long, err, I'll call you, oh
right, yes, can I have your mobile, mine's disappeared err,
I've, well, I don't know, given it away or something, anyway,
can I have your mobile? Otherwise I can't call you and that
would be silly because the two of us, you and me, we belong
together, Kay, err Stefan err Hans? Karsten? Friedrich? Lars?
Nils? Jörg? Ludwig? Peter? Or, err, what was your name
again, it slipped my mind for a minute, sorry, won't happen
again, oh, huh, now I've, shit, fuck, I put the four billion in my
jeans by mistake and they're, oh shit, in the washing machine
and oh dear, well, err, I mean, sorry, could you help me out
again otherwise I'll have to cancel Johannes and Max again
and that err would be kind of awkward, five, six billion, that
should be enough, that'll see me through to next week, great,
thanks, you're an absolute angel, this time I won't leave the
money in the taxi by mistake or tip it down the incinerator
by mistake, I don't know how that happened, I thought it was
the biodegradable waste but I guess it wasn't, sorry, won't
happen again, so, okay, bye-bye, kiss-kiss, and yes, but, err,
what did I want to, oh yes, don't forget me, right, I love you,
well, so long and oh right, one more thing, I'm kind of oh god,
sorry about this, but don't be surprised if, well, if, err, if the
doorbell rings tomorrow or the day after tomorrow or maybe
they won't come till the day after the day after tomorrow, but
the flat, I've, well, I've sold the flat or actually I've sublet it or
actually I told my parents they could stay here for a while or
actually I did all of those things and told my sister she could
store her furniture here, she's going abroad for a couple of
years and err, don't be surprised, I don't know who'll ring the
doorbell first but I sold the flat to err seven different buyers
yesterday and they've all given me the down payment in
cash and I'm using the money to go on holiday with Michael
or Matthias or both, I just need to get away for a bit, it's so
stressful here, I need a bit of quiet, then I'll feel better and I
won't be so touchy and we'll get along better I JUST NEED
TO RELAX A BIT AND TO CALM DOWN and then I can

concentrate on the two of us again, so leave your new address
for me somewhere and then in two months everything will
be great again between the two of us, okay darling, I love you
and one last time, you can trust me, honest, I've changed, you
can trust me, I'll have changed soon, when I'm back, IF I'm
back everything will be the way it was or err no, not at all,
everything will be completely different, it'll be great, so: so
long, darling, I love you. Oh, and if you go out, err, don't be
surprised, the tram and the hospital and the, err, water supply
company, I've done a very clever cross-border leasing deal
or whatever it's called and lent them to Shanghai via Poland
and the Ukraine, and if you want to take the train you have to
err buy it back first and then buy a ticket, I hope that's okay,
your bank advisor can explain all of it if he's still there, i.e. *it's*
still there, the bank, because it's in on the deal and if it crashes
then it'll be gone too, I mean the town in which you err live
or not, so if it seems as if everyone around you is speaking
Chinese that could be err that could be because they are, I
mean they could actually be speaking Chinese because they've
taken over, taken this scrap heap, and then it would be good
if you could learn quickly, I mean Chinese, so you could at
least ask for directions now and then so you don't get lost, oh
shit, fuck, my God, I've just remembered they were planning
to build this dam here, tomorrow or something, no, today,
oh yes, right, in a minute, here, in two minutes or in one or
something they'll blow all this up and wash it away, they need
energy, they just need more energy, oh God, you should try
and err somehow get away, but where, well, aah, who knows,
no idea, and with what, think of something, darling, okay then,
bye-bye, see you around, the question is where and in what
condition, well, okay, I'll be going, I, err, I'll be, bye-bye, off.

Collapses

I think I'll just collapse now.

I think I'll just collapse now too.

Me too.

The Great Bark

Go ahead and bark, go ahead and bark... really loud, angry, aggressive

Meow, meow

No, go ahead and bark, really bark

Meow meow

No, imagine you're angry, you've had it, you've HAD ENOUGH say NOW I'VE HAD ENOUGH

Now I've had enough

Yes, but say it like you mean it

What?

Say it like you mean it

Mean what?

That you've had it, that you've heard enough lies, that you won't be fucked with any more, that if they think they can push you around they've got another thing coming

Oh right

I'VE HAD ENOUGH

(Laughs.)

I'VE FINALLY HAD ENOUGH!! I'M PUTTING A STOP TO THIS RIGHT NOW

(Laughs.) yes, I see

and then bark, just go ahead and bark

(Barks very quietly.)

aggressive, loud, angry, as if you're about to beat everything to a pulp. Now the whole group, aggressive, loud, angry, as if you've now reached the point where you've had it, where you won't have the piss taken any more, WHERE YOU'VE HAD ENOUGH, go ahead and bark, now bark, BARK!

(Everyone barks but very quietly, it's more of a whimper, a very cautious lapdog bark.)

FOR GOD'S SAKE, YOU'RE MEANT TO BARK, YOU MORONS

(A quiet, feeble bark that partly turns into an uncertain cough.)

BARK, GO ON, BARK, YOU'VE HAD ENOUGH, YOU DON'T WANT THIS ANYMORE, YOU WON'T BE PUSHED AROUND ANYMORE you're about to beat everything and everyone to a pulp, you're going into this bank and you're going to grab the first banker you see and whack his fucking mug onto the in-tray on his fucking counter and make him eat those fucking worthless fund papers and hit his head against the fucking ad poster that promises endless returns hanging on the wall next to him until he throws up and vomits blood until slime drools from his stupid lying mug and he's begging and whining and pleading for mercy and screaming and then you leave that piece of shit there and move on to the next one, keep following the hierarchy, higher and higher *(He stops, looks around, looks into puzzled faces.)*

14 Years / 3 Weeks – I

I've never really

what

I've never really oh I don't know I suppose

what is it, what

to be honest I've never really

yes

do you want me to be honest

yes please

never really

yes

found you that interesting

(Pause.)

I mean you were just there. And sometimes you weren't, sometimes we talked, sometimes we didn't, I wouldn't say that... but I don't want to hurt your feelings, it was all such a long time ago

To me it doesn't really

it was all such a long time ago, I'm someone different now and all that was a completely different life

three weeks

what?

it was three weeks ago. Three weeks ago I got up and all your things had gone. And then I just sat there and waited, for hours, days, just waited, but you'd gone.

that's what I said, it was a long time ago and sometimes at night I watched you when you were sleeping and then you were like, how shall I put it, like the wardrobe or, even better, like the radio that was playing quietly somewhere in the background, someone had left it on in the background, it was a kind of hiss, a kind of incidental, elusive hiss and

Fourteen years

what?

Fourteen years, that's how long we were together

(Pause.)

oh really, it was that long? My God.

(Pause.)

I didn't really... my God *(laughs)* realise. Fourteen years and... but that was all ages ago

three weeks, three weeks, that's how long it's been, three weeks ago I got up and you'd gone and I walked through the flat looking for you but there was nothing left, nothing, no sign, no message, you'd simply gone

II

I'm like Money

The trust is gone. And I have to direct my anger at something,
I can't buy myself a Che Guevara t-shirt at Prada every time
I'm angry and strut down the Ku Damm in it, I have to find
a way to direct my anger at something so I can feel that
THINGS ARE CHANGING, and not just the things you
have to buy.

All I can do is change my style, that's all I can change, now
and then I can exchange my body with someone else, but
even that only works for a day or two, then he moves onto
another body, why not, these bodies are all standardized, he
might as well take another body, he DOESN'T SEE THE
DIFFERENCE that I keep trying to create, MY ATTEMPTS
TO CREATE A DIFFERENCE ARE TOO TIMID, I need
to be MORE BRAVE but I haven't made up my mind yet,
I haven't FOUND A DIRECTION, I stay the same and it
makes me sick that I stay the same

YESTERDAY I BOUGHT THIS BLOUSE AT ESCADA
it's very pretty, isn't it? BUT MY LIFE HASN'T CHANGED
BECAUSE OF IT, I'M STILL THE SAME I'm exactly the
same and I'm not really here, I'm still kind of a child whose
parents left it fourteen years ago in a hotel room in Hong
Kong or Beijing or Shanghai on a business trip or promo
tour or whatever, ON THE RUN FOR TAX EVASION,
in the Pacific Ocean, and I'm still sitting here and everyone
is speaking Chinese and is quite nice but I don't understand
anything and no one talks to me and I keep waiting for my
parents to come back and get me or to send someone to pick
me up for or a message from them so I have something to
go on I HAVE NOTHING TO GO ON, I just don't, I'M
LIKE MONEY damn, I'm like money, I'm everything and
everywhere and no one can gauge my value

and every day you have to check if I'm still worth something because it changes every day, my worth, my relationship to other people, and I'm in constant danger of becoming worthless over night, I'm in constant danger of collapsing,

I'M LIKE MONEY, everyone wants me and lots of it but I don't manage to make anyone happy

even if that's what they think,

and I can go anywhere, I can no longer gauge my value because there are no longer any guidelines, they're in the process of disintegrating,

I'M LIKE MONEY,

that's nice too, because there's money everywhere and it knows no borders,

no morals and no fear,

sometimes it's shy when you ask it to provide collateral and then it prefers to withdraw, or if it's supposed to step in when there's an emergency, when it's supposed to help others it would rather walk away and that's what I do too, I prefer to LEAVE VERY QUICKLY when it matters,

it's getting too risky with you, darling, you're nice and cute but at the moment there are more lucrative markets elsewhere

YOU JUST WANT TOO MUCH and I can't give it to you, I have to PROTECT my resources FOR GOD'S SAKE now my Pradaskirt has got tangled in my Escadablouse and ALL THESE IMAGE CONSTRUCTS have suddenly got tangled

no one can stand what functions as "I" in this trust,

fuck it, I earn 200 000 a year and sometimes they pay me so it's two millions in STOCKS AND BONDS but I can't cash them because then the stock market would crash as well and then the company I work for and that I part-own wouldn't be worth anything and then I'd be unemployed and then I can FORGET THE BONDS sometimes I'm just gone for a bit, just gone, for example everyone put such great hopes in me to change my life so they'd have a great future ahead of them, but then I just left, you're such a dear little bunny-rabbit my darling, but you're living in the wrong country, yes, sorry, it's just not working for me.

So what now, what now, I should keep going but my body's kind of stuck here, it's moving through time and space with great freedom and speed but I keep getting stuck here, it's a strange feeling, I'm everywhere but I'm stuck to my clothes in this place and I'm getting more and more stiff, it's strange, I'm no longer moving yet I keep going from place to place, and I no longer feel the need for anything, I'm here now, I can stay.

I'm so glad you're finally gone

My God, I was so bored with you, you can't imagine. In the morning, when you were lying next to me or when you were pulling your trolley case through the living room for hours because you hadn't realised you were in my flat and not some crappy airport where you had to run up and down so people wouldn't think you'd fallen into some kind of paralysis out of fear, or when you had NOTHING for dinner because your body is about to fall apart from exhaustion and lack of strength and you have to keep punishing it for that, your BODYCONTAINER, my God, it was all so boring, you can't imagine, I fell asleep every time you were drunk and crashed into a pram in slow motion at five in the morning doing forty kilometres an hour and I had to come pick you up from the hospital, God, it took time and strength and it was so dull, my God, so dull. I'm so glad you're finally gone, that you're finally gone

14 Years/ 3 Weeks – II

You're confusing, I mean I don't know, but you're somehow getting things mixed up here

What

Fourteen years ago we spent three weeks

No

Yes, trust me, fourteen years ago we spent three weeks together, but that's all such a long time ago now and I can't even really remember it anymore, I heard you got married or something

Yes, to you

No, no, you're wrong there, at least I don't, I mean I don't know, suddenly you'd gone, were just gone, that's what I heard, you'd suddenly

Yes, because you left, I mean, you were suddenly gone, all your things had gone and I was suddenly on my own, I mean after fourteen years, and then I, I just, oh I don't know

Yes, you see, you can't remember any of it any more, it's all such a long time ago

Three weeks, it was three weeks ago, three weeks ago I got up and everything was quiet and I looked around and all your things had gone and everything had changed, suddenly everything was completely different and you'd suddenly gone

That's fourteen years ago now, I'm sorry, fourteen years ago we spent three weeks together but it was kind of, I mean it was nice and all that, but it was kind of nothing, nothing important, at least not to me, I abandoned that project pretty quickly and then for the next fourteen years you'd, I don't know, disappeared? That's what I heard, you'd disappeared, you'd gone

No

Yes, I think

No

Yes, I think, to be honest, yes, I'm sorry

We were together

Yes I know but not really, not properly, it was just, I'm sorry.

Three Weeks

It was three weeks ago

Three weeks ago I got up and suddenly

Everything was quiet

You couldn't hear anything

All your things had gone

And I sat down

And for the first time in my life I heard

This silence

This calm

And that

That's okay too

That's okay

That you'd just gone

And then it was quiet

And calm

And then I went and stood by the window

And I looked out

And I saw the city lights

And everything slowed down

Way down

And then it got dark

And I stayed by the window the whole time and didn't move
and looked out

night after night and it was nice

It was so calm

And then the phone rang and I knew it was you

You wanted to explain everything

But I didn't care

And then I searched through the flat looking for stuff you'd left behind

But there was nothing, it was all gone

And since then I just sit there

Day after day

I just stand by the window and don't move

And look out

And I know you're out there somewhere

Somewhere but I don't need to see you

Or meet you

It's enough that I know you're out there somewhere and you call me now and then

I don't even have to answer the phone

It's enough that I know that you call me now and then and I don't even have to talk to you and I stand there

And it's completely quiet and I don't hear your voice

And I don't hear your breathing

And you don't tell me what you did all day

you don't come to me at night and want to hold me or want me to hold you or want to tell me something, you're just gone, you're just gone and it's quiet and it's nice and then I just sit there and I know that I could be anywhere but I'm here now

and there are people that want to see me but I refuse to see
them and there are people that want to be with me but I don't
want to be with them I just stay here

It's so nice

So quiet

I could be anywhere now but I'm not

Maybe I just stand by the window and don't move.

I used to want to change the world

I used to want to change the world and now I'm just caring about parking place.

I used to want to change the world but I forgot what that meant.

I used to want to change the world and then I met you.

I used to want to change the world and then my father died.

I used to want to change the world and now I just want to join it.

I used to want to change the world and now I just want to move in it.

I used to want to change the world and then I started to walk around and got lost.

I used to want to change the world and then I forgot what I wanted.

I used to want to change the world until I figured out what the world really is.

I used to want to change the world so much that I never stopped.

I used to want to change the world I started changing so much I didn't know who I was.

The Island of unused, unloved Bodies

And everything was quiet and I kept walking, on and on, and then suddenly everything was gone and no one and nothing was left, inside me, and I kept walking and walking and suddenly I was on this island of unloved, exhausted bodies that disappear into the fog and dissolve into the horizon like a sketch in pencil and everything got slower and slower, there was no noise, everything just lay there, forever, in the fog, waiting for me forever, and there were just these exhausted, unused bodies slowly stroking their skin with their hands, no one said anything and everyone lay there and everything got slower and slower and I could hear my own breathing and I don't know how long I'd been lying there and I couldn't see an end to it, everything kept going and going and going and going but everything stayed the same and I felt nothing and heard nothing and I saw myself, saw myself slowly, in slow motion, sinking to the ground and I stayed there and nothing happened and there was no thought, no memory, just the fog, and everything dissolved and I was lying by the water in the fog and had stopped moving, I was breathing and I knew: I'm here now. This is what I've become. This. This. This. This.

And if I told you

And if I told you it wouldn't change anything

And if I didn't tell you it wouldn't change anything

And if I loved you it wouldn't change anything

And it we stayed together it wouldn't change anything

And if I packed my bags it wouldn't change anything

And if I call you it doesn't change anything

And if I don't call you it doesn't change anything

And if I kiss you it doesn't change anything

And if I really, really want you it doesn't change anything

And if I, if I fall asleep now it doesn't change anything

(Pause.)

And if I leave it doesn't change anything

And if I just stand by the window it doesn't change anything

And if I just say yes for once it doesn't change anything

And if I just understand you for one minute it doesn't change anything

And if I trust you, if I, when I

And when I

When I

I just can't

I just

What is this? but I

If I

If

And if I

If I

O my God

I really can't do this

I'm so sorry

Forget what I said

I'm sorry

I'm so sorry

I didn't mean it

Let's just leave things the way they are

Let's not mess everything up

All this has taken so long

It was so so

Exhausting

It's only about me

It's not about you

Somehow it's in me and

This is all my

This is all my, I mean this is

O God

This is me

And this is you

O God

And I

I can't do this

And if I touch you it doesn't change anything

And if I really, really want you it doesn't change anything

O God

But let's just leave things the way they are

Contracts of Employment

I keep meeting these good-looking interesting young energetic
men and I want to have some kind of relationship with them,
I mean I'd like to discuss art with them, listen to music,
have a long snog, sleep with them, but they keep asking for
contracts, they all want contracts of employment, they want
to work for me and have a contract, at least some money,
benefits, something they can get a bit more out of than a few
nice hours (those hours are only nice for me since the young
men pay in their currency, their youth, their youthful energy,
their beautiful bodies, their fresh view of this world and this
market.) And what about me? I have to repay them somehow,
and above all this generation needs structure, contracts of
employment or simply money since they want to buy things
or go away or have a computer so they can access the net,
they can't keep going from one internship to the next, they've
all studied art history and literature and media design and
the cultural history of Tibet and now they're standing next
to photocopiers and taking envelopes to the post office, they
want more than just lying around, listening to music and
snogging.

14 Years / 3 Weeks – III

Now I remember. We spent three weeks together in the past fourteen years, I've worked it all out, listed the days, the times, the moments we spent together, I've written it all down and calculated, I mean I've worked it all, down to, I've noted, you see, here, look at this and there, yes, look

14.7.2006 11.53 until 12.03 and

21.11.2007 9.13 until 10.24

we spent three weeks together in the past fourteen years and I've put you in my

just leave me alone, okay, I mean you're nice and all that but please just leave me alone, I haven't got any, I mean I just can't, and, you know, I'm sorry, but leave me be, thanks

Confessions

<u>The Boy</u>

Maybe you should have been there now and then

You were always gone

I'm not angry with you or anything

I mean how could I be, I don't even know you, but

Somehow

I'm fine and

I get by

I don't think I have any whatever, any traumas or disorders

I mean I don't know how you could have caused them

We don't know each other

But

You shouldn't have just taken off like that

<u>The Girl</u>

Fourteen years ago I woke up and suddenly everything was quiet

And suddenly you'd gone

And at reception no one knew where you were either

So I just stayed in this room

For the next few years

You'd left some money but

It was somewhere in Shanghai on the 27th floor and

I mean I was four

And for fourteen years I simply didn't leave the hotel room

I sat there

Watched TV

The Chinese had this programme where they showed explosions the whole time

They kept blowing up buildings

That's what they showed

So I decided to become an explosives expert

Not for buildings

But for financial products

The Boy

Maybe you just should have been here and now and then

More than three weeks a year

You were just gone

I was fourteen and you just left

You left me there

Were suddenly gone

Everything was quiet

My whole childhood was so incredibly quiet and silent and

The Woman

I'm not sure who you are, but

The Man

You're hallucinating

The Woman

I don't even know you

The Boy

Yes, how would you, you just left

The Woman

Well, maybe I was busy, but

The Boy

Mum, I was four years old.

The Woman

Don't call me mum, I don't like it, and anyway, it's not your turn, it's Nina's turn

Nina, what would you like to say?

The other Girl

Me, nothing

The Woman

But it's your turn

The other Girl

But I don't want to say anything

The Woman

But it's your turn

The other Girl

But I don't want to

The Man

But it's your turn, my God

The Boy

Well if Nina doesn't want to say anything then maybe I could, mum, I

The Woman

It's not your turn. It's Nina's turn. Nina, say something

The Man

Say something

The other Girl

No

The Man

Say anything

The other Girl

No, I don't want to

The Girl

Just say something, doesn't matter what

The other Girl

But I don't have anything to say

The Girl

It's all right

The Man

Go on and say something

The Woman

Are you all right?

The other Girl

What?

The Man

Are you all right?

The other Girl

Yes, I think, I suppose, yes, right?

The Woman

Tell us a bit more

The other Girl

I don't know.

The Woman

Are you all right?

The Man

Are you

The Woman

In trouble?

The other Girl

Me?

The Man

Go on, my god, how difficult can it be

(Pause.)

The other Girl

I don't know, no, no idea, I don't know if anything is wrong,
if anything should be different, maybe, I'm not sure, actually
I think I'm all right but you can never really tell if that's
enough or if there's something I'm not even aware of yet, so…
yes, I just don't know, I can't tell, I keep looking and looking
but I can't find anything in me that is really, really troubling
me, actually I think everything is all right, but maybe we could
find something that we could work on together, some kind of
disorder or something, there has to be something, no one is
happy, that just doesn't exist, that's why I don't trust myself,
there has to be something in me that… something that…

Maybe you stand by the Window and don't move

Maybe you stand by the window and don't move and I hold onto you

I search for your eyes but I can't find them

Maybe I've forgotten everything

Maybe I don't discover anything

And maybe you stand by the window and don't move and I don't see you

III

Landscapes waiting for a Meltdown

An endless golf course

It sits there

quietly

only the sound of the sprinkler

which for years has provided this living bunker by the sea with
its twenty-seven golf courses and 13728 three-and-a-half room
luxury apartments with water every half hour

he looks around

there's no one here

not a soul anywhere

everything is quiet

apart from the continually returning sound of the sprinkler

no one here plays golf

no one lives here

a landscape waiting to rise in value

Seventeen per cent of 1400 of these flats belong to the
retirement fund which he has bought shares in since 2004 with
four per cent of his monthly income

and this money is sitting here

and is growing

and is growing and secure and

everything is quiet

Stefan is getting restless

Goes and stands by the window

But there's nothing to see

The last fourteen pages of the last chapter of his book LIFE IN CRISIS CHAPTER 27: MONEY PREFERS TO LIVE ON WITHOUT US financial streams and the erosion of the self are lying on his desk

After the neoliberal economic systems had taken the formerly democratic governments allocated to them hostage, they were able to steer the national and international financial streams and to determine the sums that were then transferred to them.

Can't concentrate, goes to the kitchen

The government's task is to organise the approval of the masses

Makes himself a cup of tea

States becoming banks was preceded by banks becoming state banks

resistance?

What, in a financial democracy, can actually be influenced by elections and what is completely beyond the influence of the voter

Is there anger somewhere

in me

out there

A notice in the paper

During an unregistered demonstration Chinese workers lynch one of the managers that has driven their factory to bankruptcy and made them unemployed

They'd simply had it

in France redundant workers threaten to blow up their factory.

He looks out the window

Everything is still quiet

And they keep asking us to take China as an example

So why don't we

If they don't like something they freak out and hit people until their skulls are lying smashed in front of them

They're not as nice as us

I can't buy a Che Guevara t-shirt every time I'm angry and I don't like something and walk up and down the street in it. That's no longer enough to realise my goals

Judith reaches the 27th floor of the large conference hotel holding a suitcase containing 200 million euros

27th floor, a slight headache

What is it that's calming all of us down, why are we always so incredibly calm, he goes and stands by the window, screaming children,

The money has to go, it mustn't grow any more or work for me in secret, it has to be EXCHANGED for LIFE

chapter 27: is resistance possible? and if yes, how?

Stefan returns to his desk

lea stands behind a large glass pane

no sound

she switches on the television: explosions

When I was a child I kept watching these films on television that showed buildings being blown up, I always really liked those

When everything sinks to the ground

Everything collapses

I wanted to do that too

Make things collapse

She's had this strange talent

Ever since she was a child

She sees all these networks

Like people that see the number pi as a colour

Speak twenty languages

Or are able to divide 5723 by 2,783 just like that and can tell you the correct result including 200 figures after the comma

When a fund collapses she can see who was connected to this large network, who has crashed and lost everything

And that gives her pleasure

Seeing them all lying there

Unable to get back up

Yesterday all of this was still a great promise of endless riches

The maximisation of profit

Money without work

And now all this has disappeared

And no one knows why

Everything is lying there

These unpredictable collapses

So quiet

Stefan goes to the basement and searches for a book in an old box

He can no longer remember which of those rooms is his basement and in which box he put the books

Stands undecided for a moment

If I bet that between 14.34 and 14.35 Tokyo time counter insurance for a credit insurance will drop in value by 2.4 per cent – because a student in Oregon who takes out a loan and on 14.5.2007 uses it to buy four houses in Ford Laughterdale and on 12.10.2008 sells them with a 3 per cent profit per house in order to finance an advertising campaign for his newly-founded company that advises ailing insurance companies, then

She sees all these networks

She is sitting in her hotel room on the 27th floor behind this glass pane and looks at the charts on her laptop

And the numbers and letters of all these funds are connected to names and networks

She knows who invested what percentage

All this money

crackles

sets people into motion

collapses

There is beauty in these collapses

She leans back, closes her eyes and enjoys these silent collapses

Crash

The sound of breathing

The crackling of these rows of numbers

inaudible

All the drama hiding behind them

fear

anger

screams

loss

She takes the papers and puts them away and repacks them and repacks them again and sees

sees Kay walking across deserted gold courses framing the coast of Spain

Landscapes waiting to collapse

And she sees judith, who travels the world with all her money in cash and without

investments in funds to find out what money can set in motion if it's not frozen or parked somewhere, what happens when money suddenly meets real people who would do anything to get it, even simulate emotions and intensity,

money can do a lot more than wait in a fund until it collapses.

She's lying on the bed in her hotel room surrounded by sixteen million people

And I don't know yet where I'm going to go from here

Everything is so quiet here

Once a month the investors, mainly pensioners from Germany, the Netherlands, Scandinavia and Florida, meet and walk across the golf course to the expansive pavilion, there's a karaoke party

No one here plays golf

It would damage the grass and prevent the property from increasing in value

No one lives here

It would wear down the property and decrease the value of the fund

And no one here wants to decrease values

Because these are the only values these people have

She checks the internet for people offering funds or web page specialists and invites them to her hotel room and lets them talk

About their lives

I want to hear stories

About people

I want to see them live again

I'm fed up with facebook and elite single.de

That crap has ruined my life

And now everything has collapsed and no one knows where it all went

Everything is gone

Because it was never there

They just pretended it existed

These banks have the power to say what exists and what doesn't, they can just say a fictional number and lend it to someone and then this sum is suddenly out there and suddenly has to be worked for by real people and this abstract figure becomes a real value. But when the real value is a bet which I trace back to a student in Oregon whom I granted a credit over two million dollars between 17.13 on October 12 and 17.50 on October 13 so he could take an option on the three per cent decline of a number of counter-insured fund papers from an insurance against credit failings in the property market of the Detroit suburbs, in this transaction between 17.18 on October 12 and 17.22 on October 12. And if I lose twelve million euro and about 3000 other players lose a similarly high sum on the same day and the bank is no longer solvent and has to get the money from the government in order to keep giving away fictitious numbers as money which

Stefan feels as if he's fallen out of the world

His friends are worried because he hasn't posted any new entries on his facebook profile for three days

What on earth is wrong, has he run out of ideas

Most people on facebook are simply better than me: they have funnier, funkier, more original lines, cooler pictures and somehow they all know heike makkatsch and benno führmann and some of them are even cross-linked to quentin tarantino and I only know 20% of the people who are my friends and they're all just unemployed actors, drama students or my parents. And that makes me feel like a loser.

I have to keep being original here and that's really hard work I CAN'T BE FUNNY AND ORIGINAL ALL THE TIME, this pressure to perform, I have to keep advertising myself with each sentence I speak into this room teeming with other image constructs, I have to advertise myself as a product and I JUST CAN'T DO IT ANYMORE

27th floor, a slight headache.

I'm starting to get hot… I feel this, I felt it right away: this closeness, right? You and me. The two of us. Together. We really click, we have a long road ahead of us, together, the next few years, I mean, there's chemistry between us, Mrs err, what? You're such an inspiring, fun-loving, curious, attractive, spontaneous, adventurous, active, unconventional, sociable, sensitive, understanding, fresh, sporty, individual, youthful, creative, entertaining, buoyant, passionate, sensible, sensitive, flexible … did you say 200 million?

Yes, my husband…

Oh right

Yes, don't worry *(laughs)*, he no longer exists, only in the shape of these 200 million and they ... have to go away now, look after them... take off the rest, darling, forestry did you say?

do you know what Busso count of Schulenburg and his son Bolko, who have been active in the US forestry industry for many years, always say?

All of it

Wood growth is independent of economic booms and crises.

That's important: growth is independent of crises.

Yes, and that's exactly what I can offer you.

That's important. I've had so many crises in the past few years you wouldn't believe. And nothing has grown. I mean the man was so exhausted and empty, just like all those products he keeps rebundling and repackaging and selling on the web, it was bound to collapse at some point. He kept collapsing, every night, here in my arms, it was only a matter of time before the market followed suit. I mean I have a huge need to catch up on some very, very substantial

I really can offer you all of that. Substantiality is my specialty. I'm always very, very substantial. What kind of investor are you?

Lonely

vulnerable

Very, very disappointed in the market

But ready to give everything.

She's lying on her bed watching these men who are slowly stripping and she realises: this is a good investment. These men are very sensitive and they really give everything because she has something everyone is looking for: money

The way everything here is slowly collapsing, it's so beautiful, this fear in the eyes of all these men, who now for the first time feel their lives

Did they really think that they could endlessly keep pushing these zero values?

Now here he is in the wellness palais of the golf colony that was built expansively round the Spanish coast with tax money and takes the microphone for his first karaoke song, but

In this corner of the world there seems to be no energy left in people's bodies

They no longer know in which direction to move and

Oh it's you, oh God, I know you

Yes, we were married once

Well, then the rest of the evening's programme is sorted, well, come on in, this is bound to be a sore disappointment. Do we really have to talk before we have sex?

Well, that's what we agreed on the profile

All right, you start, but don't go on too long, I have to work tonight, I wanted a bit of distraction, wear that cap so I won't see you that clearly when you're lying on top of me, or can we get the sex over with first and then talk, would that be possible, I think I'd prefer that, or we could just talk online later, I'm not really the communicative type

Aha but in your profile you said

Yes darling, but you're not exactly the twenty-nine-year-old parachutist I was expecting either, so let's get down to business before I start to

quiet

This corridor is quiet

It's the moment before she enters the room

Her mother ran away with all the money

somewhere

200 million

She no longer wants to invest it, she finally wants to spend it

She's finally exchanging it for a life

With people and feelings

Her father has retired to his home in Spain

All he does is play golf and sing karaoke

Her boyfriend hasn't been in touch for weeks

He's lying in the basement somewhere writing a book about resistance

Meticulously collecting everything he can find

Short eruptions of anger

Cars set on fire

Beaten-up fund advisors

Murdered factory owners

All over the world

Burning bank branches

Everything here is quiet

still

Now they're coming through the door

We don't really have a relationship except that you're my boyfriend but apart from that: I rarely see you, I barely know you, so I've been thinking that

No, stop right there

I'm leaving

no

yes

I can't live like this anymore. It's like… not being alive.
Whether you're there or not or whether I'm here or not…
it all feels the same and… I need to leave, I want to change
this… I want… a different life

2 a.m.

27th floor

A slight headache

Kay looks across the endless golf course. The entire Spanish
coast is lined by gold course after golf course and the sun is
sinking

not a sound, just the sprinkler

At this moment judith is standing by the window and not
moving

Sixteen million people

and I don't belong

Stefan is lying in the basement between the boxes of his
collapsed bookshelves

200 second hand books about resistance and revolutionary
energies are lying on top of him and are suffocating him

He feels this energy

all these thoughts

this urge to think differently about things

to overthrow them

to restructure them

but he can't move

lea looks at the monitor

the parcels for the retirement fund for 1400 luxury apartments by the Spanish coast

are lying on front of her

She has bundled the parcels

Bundled, rebundled, repacked

Like small time bombs these parcels are ticking

I wanted to be an explosives expert

Even as a child

Not for buildings

But for financial products

I bundled the fund parcels and rebundled them again and again and put very unobtrusive timers on them

And no branch manager of any bank has any idea of what's in these parcels

I knew

One day it'll all blow up

I sat there

Very calmly

In my Credit Suisse office in Shanghai

And put these small, unobtrusive packages together

That promised a return of seventeen per cent within the first six months

And they worked

But in the seventh month

Everything collapsed

Everything

And all these greedy stupid pigs choked on the ruins of fund systems that had become fucking worthless

And I heard them gasping

And calling for help

And if they hadn't been so clever as to make sure that their governments simply reimbursed all their losses with so-called emergency parachutes and emergency reserves we would finally have been rid of all these useless greedy pigs

They would lie there

Weakly

Calling for help

And slowly choking on their greed and their stupidity

That's how the last chapter of Stefan's book MONEY PREFERS TO LIVE ON WITHOUT US ends and it ended up turning into a kind of story or short prose text

A kind of essay or collection of texts

I never entirely settled on a form

Since every chapter demanded a new style of writing

The anger was there and got lost again

And in the end he was lying there

quietly

this

this

this is me

my life

now

here

everything comes to a standstill

(Pause.)

Everything comes to a standstill

And I don't know where I'm going to go from here

SOLO SWIM

Slight headache
2 a.m.
all calm
not sure in which direction I wanna move from here

27th floor
tall glass walls

full protection (all my life)

and there are people who want to see me
but there's no one I want to see

27th floor
tall glass walls
everything quiet
there are no sounds up here

I could be anywhere
But I am not

The water has stopped moving
Sixteen million people

and all of this is bigger than I could ever be
and all of this is bigger than I will ever be

everything has become so safe in these past few years

everything has become so safe

I am guided by an electronic navigating system that tells me exactly where to go

Guides me from outer space to absolute precision

All these options and possibilities

I can never go wrong

Never offroads

I always arrive
I always arrive

All these years precisely mapped out for me

Someone must have been there before me

Someone must have been there before me doing all the research and I am following what they have come up with

What a scary feeling thinking of all the years ahead of me

Maybe if I stop to listen

Maybe if I hold my breath

2 a.m.

Slight dizziness

All lights shut down

Blinking

Driving

Heavy dark ships

27th floor

no sound from the outside

Somewhere someone is waiting for me

But I don't want to get in contact

Somewhere someone is waiting for me

To start the day with a smile

Throw some eggs in the pan make some phone calls

take my little girls to school and go to work

be good be creative be inspired be inspiring

come up with new ideas come up with something totally new that has never been done the new hot thing the ultimate in movement full of brilliant ideas thought and concept yet so free and straight from all my heart and instinct and yet a lasting experience that is wholly and spiritual and funny and serious and breath taking and hilarious and sexy and smooth and radical, cutting edge and accessible, personal, deep, beautiful and universal, challenging, subversive and emotional, slightly anarchistic, very, very entertaining ABSOLUTELY MAKES SENSE and FUCKING SELLS pick up the girls from school drive them to my mother's house, can you watch over them? Keep them busy? Steve and I have to focus on that new concept applying for another grant you know you see well sorry well no, you cant go for yoga for one day then Mom, for chrisssake PLEASE why are you being so difficult Lisa, Lisa, you are staying with Grandma today and yes, yes, please, Lisa, Sophie, hey, please, hey, come on, WHAT? Drive Lisa back as she caught a fever put her to bed, read stories, wait for the babysitter, go to the pharmacist, buy medicine, make her tea, yes, yes, these girls are all I want in life, they are bigger than life, Steve and I have to focus on this thing again, must be written in a way that they will give us more money, must be written in a way that THIS WHOLE DAMN SHOW CAN GO ON

All this comes to a standstill

I could be anywhere

But I am not

I could be anywhere now

Behind high glass walls soundproof and secure

And I don't know how I got here

So calm clear clean and full of knowledge about myself

Everything slows down

My life my fears my family and how I can work things out

It scares me

All these first aid kits I have in my head

The water has stopped moving

Whenever we have an argument we sit down and talk and soon we sort things out.

Everything has become so secure

So clear

I just have to enter where I want to go and that's where I arrive

This building is so secure

I cannot leave

I can only collapse

All has come to standstill

And then slowly

Very slowly

I start to move

While no one is watching
Ignore all instructions
Ignore all wisdom
All doors in flight
Take off no landing

27th floor

high glass walls

everything is quiet

and I don't know where I'm going to go from here

everything is so safe

everything has become so safe these past few years

I keep following the navigation system which tells me exactly
where to go

a highly complex system of possibilities and options

and all I have to do is enter where I want to go

and then that's where I arrive

someone must have been here before me and recorded
everything

and all I have to do is follow the instructions

and then I arrive

I always arrive

I always arrive

I keep following this navigation system and then I arrive

a highly complex system of roads and options and possibilities

and all I have to do is enter where I want to go

and then that's where I arrive

I always arrive

all these possibilities

and I just keep following this electronic navigation system

someone must have been here before me and recorded all
these roads

and all I have to do is enter where I want to go

and then that's where I arrive

27th floor

a slight headache

everything slows down

Sixteen million people

and I don't know how I got here

everyone is so nice to me

they're all so nice to me

if I need something I make a phone call and then I get it

everything has become so safe these past few years, so straight,
so clear

clear and easy to understand

this building offers me protection

no sounds

no sound reaches up here

the river flows more slowly

the lights

night-time

everything is quiet

no sound

Sixteen million people

I could be anywhere now

but I'm here

everything has become so safe these past few years

everything is so

I keep following the navigation system and

I always arrive

I always arrive

everything has become so safe

27th floor

2 a.m.

a slight headache

16 million people

high glass walls

I don't know how I got here

if I need something I make a phone call and then I get it

everything has become so safe these past few years, so straight, so clear

clear and easy to understand

I just keep following the navigation system

a highly complex system of roads and options and possibilities

and all I have to do is enter where I want to go

and the system tells me exactly how to get there

We were hardly aware of each other

All these years

Sometimes it was nice but

You weren't even here

And I wasn't here either

We weren't present

We weren't here

We weren't

We weren't we

We were just the argument about what we weren't

All that comes to a halt

2 a.m.

and I don't know where I'm going to go from here

everything comes to a halt

and I don't know where I'm going to go from here

everything has become so safe these past few years

everything is so

I always arrive

I always arrive

everything has become so safe

27th floor

2 a.m.

a slight headache

Sixteen million people

I don't know how I got here

everyone is so nice to me

they're all so nice to me

if I need something I make a phone call and then i get it

everything has become so safe these past few years, so straight, so clear

clear and easy to understand

I just keep following the navigation system

a highly complex system of roads and options and possibilities

and all I have to do is enter where I want to go

and the system tells me exactly how to get there

thousands of roads and streets and

I know exactly which way I have to go

and I always arrive

someone must have been here before me and recorded everything

and all I have to do is follow

I always arrive

I always arrive

everything is so safe

and I don't know where I'm going to go from here

everything is so quiet

everything is so still

Sixteen million people

tall glass walls

no sounds

all these roads

someone must have been here before me and recorded
everything

everything has been described, noted, written down

and all I have to do is follow the instructions

I just keep following the navigation system

it's so nice here

I always arrive

2 a.m., a slight headache

and then I arrive

and I don't know where I'm going to go from here

everything is so quiet

and I don't know how i got here

but now I'm here

it all happened so fast

and I can't remember anything

high glass walls

and maybe I just stood there by the window and didn't move

everything has become so safe these past few years

someone must have been here before me

who recorded everything

here I am

I could be anywhere

but I'm not

I'm here

and I don't know how i got here

but I'm here now

everything is quiet

tall glass windows

a slight headache

and I don't know where I'm going to go from here

I know exactly what I have to do

and I just need to follow this navigations system

someone must have been before me

we carry on

we carry on

we carry on

I always arrive
I never take a wrong turn

and if I go in the wrong direction a friendly voice tells me,
they're all so nice here, so friendly, they've all become so
incredibly nice to me in the past few years, if I need something
I get it, and if I take a wrong turn then I'm corrected only
a few seconds later, and if I throw you out the window by
mistake I just say sorry and then you forgive me, and when
I've burned 500 billion euro then I just make a call and then
someone reprints them and just gives them back and then I
can burn them again and again and again and I always get
them back, I just keep getting everything back, and I never
commit a crime, and if I do then it's just for a day or an hour
and then I'm forgiven and everything is forgotten or erased
and can start over, and when I collapse someone helps me up
and if I make everything around me collapse someone points
it out to me nicely and I'm brought to safety and put back on
track and then I keep going and make new things collapse and

I'm forgiven, I'm always forgiven, everywhere, I can do no wrong, there are these security screens everywhere and I take them down so slowly that no one notices, they cushion every impact, there is no longer any impact, everything has become so safe these past few years for me, for me it's all become so safe these past few years, I always arrive, and if everything goes up in flames I'll retire, I'll watch it from up here, up here I'm safe

www.ingramcontent.com/pod-product-compliance
Ingram Content Group UK Ltd.
Pitfield, Milton Keynes, MK11 3LW, UK
UKHW020726280225
455688UK00012B/527